Japan
Traditions and Trends

by
Carole Allen

illustrated by Ted Warren

Cover by Ted Warren

Copyright © 1992, Good Apple

ISBN No. 0-86653-684-1

Printing No. 9876543

Good Apple
1204 Buchanan St., Box 299
Carthage, IL 62321-0299

The purchase of this book entitles the buyer to reproduce student activity pages for classroom use only. Any other use requires written permission from Good Apple.

All rights reserved. Printed in the United States of America.

S I M O N & S C H U S T E R *A Paramount Communications Company*

Dedication

With much love, I dedicate this book to my husband Ed, Kim and Ray, Cindy and Jeff, and most especially, to my grandson, Tony.

Table of Contents

Copyright © 1992, Good Apple

GA1418

Books of Knowledge

Fill out this section before beginning the Japan unit.

What I know about
Japan:

What I want to learn
about Japan:

Fill out after you complete the Japan unit.

What I have learned about Japan:

Copyright © 1992, Good Apple

GA1418

Aware Square

Japanese people live in very tight quarters and have learned to be very considerate of one another. A person's feelings are very private in Japan. Generally, they place the feelings of others in front of their own. Even if someone dies, they will smile so that you will not have to look at their sad faces and feel sad, too. A person's feelings are considered seriously and sincerely. It isn't always a good idea to ask how someone feels, but perhaps you can tell by the way he acts.

When someone has a cold, often a surgical mask is worn so that no one will catch his cold.

Shopkeepers clean up the streets and sidewalks in front of their own shops and that way the shopping areas are very clean. The same is true for their homes and areas near them. Everyone does his own part.

QUESTIONS:
1. In what ways have you been taught to be considerate of others?
2. In what ways could you be more considerate of others?

ACTIVITY:
1. Prepare small squares of construction paper (2" x 3" [5.08 x 7.62 cm]) for each student in the following colors:

Red–Special Day	Green–Worried
Yellow–Happy Day	Pink–Hope for a Better Day
Blue–Sick	Purple–Sad
White–So-So	Black–Horrible

2. Have students wear squares for a week, putting them on in the morning. They may change them as the day goes on, if their moods change. No one may ask anyone why he is wearing a particular color. Someone may share with another about his feelings, if he wishes.
3. Make individual and whole class graphs and chart how the students feel in the morning.
4. Have them draw conclusions about the worst and best days of the week for them and the class.
5. Did they have good or bad days that happened to all of them at the same time?

Copyright © 1992, Good Apple

GA1418

Japan Is Born

There are many legends in Japan regarding its origins. One story tells about a god who stood on the edge of the universe with a spear in his hand. He dipped his spear into the sea and removed it. Big drops of water dropped back into the sea and these big drops became the four main islands of Japan. The smaller droplets became the 3000 smaller islands.

The celestial god and his family left heaven and went to live in these beautiful islands that are now known as Japan.

QUESTIONS:
1. How were the islands of Japan truly formed?
2. Find out what an archipelago is and name some others found around the world.

ACTIVITY:
1. Write your own clever legend about how Japan was formed.
2. Illustrate and color your story.

_____

(title)

_____

_____

_____

_____

_____

_____

_____

_____

_____

_____

Copyright © 1992, Good Apple

GA1418

Majestic Mt. Fuji

The world famous Mt. Fuji stands 12,388 feet (3716.4 m) high. It is located 100 miles (161 km) from the capital city of Tokyo, on Honshu, the main island.

During the summer thousands of people rush to climb this sacred mountain. The Japanese people fondly refer to Mt. Fuji as "Fuji-san."

Over the past several hundreds of thousands of years there have been occasional volcanic activities, and this accounts for its cone-shaped dome. Although it has been dormant for a few hundred years, the southeast slope is still classified as an active volcano.

A religious sect that combines both Buddhist and Shinto beliefs is called Fujiko. The followers of this sect climb sacred Mt. Fuji as a religious act. The mountain is divided into ten stations (gomes), from bottom to top. To walk around the rim past eight rocky peaks is known as ohachimeguri (oh-ha-chee-may-goo-ree). **Ochudo** (oh-chew-dough) means "to walk around the mountain along the fifth station line."

It is a popular sport for all people to climb Mt. Fuji. It takes about five hours to climb from the fifth station to the top. It is quite a rough hike. Many climbers use a Fuji stick to help them on their way. As they stop at each station, a special mark is made on the stick. This is taken home for a souvenir of their accomplishment. The Japanese say that it is wise to climb Mt. Fuji once in a lifetime, but it would be foolish to climb it twice.

QUESTIONS:

1. Explain what is meant by "It is wise to climb Mt. Fuji once in a lifetime, but it would be foolish to climb it twice."

   _____

   _____

2. What kinds of problems would the Japanese people experience should Mt. Fuji have a major volcanic eruption? Give an explanation for each problem.

   _____

   _____

   _____

   _____

   _____

ACTIVITY:

Prepare a list of things you would need to have in case of a major disaster in your area. Prepare a family disaster kit.

Copyright © 1992, Good Apple

GA1418

Japanese Geography

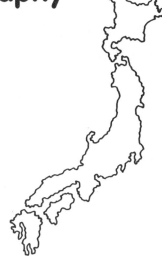

Japan is made up of four main islands. Hokkaido (hoe-kai-doe) is the second largest and most northern of the main islands. This island is underdeveloped for three reasons: it is so cold, it is made up mostly of forests and it is too far from the main island.

Honshu (hahn-shoe) is the largest and main island. Tokyo, the nation's capital, is located here. The major port and harbor of Japan is in Yokohama. Kyoto is the major cultural center of the country. Kobe is an important commercial and industrial center. All of these important cities are on the island of Honshu.

Shikoku (she-co-coo) is the smallest of the islands. It is bordered on the east by the Pacific Ocean and on the west by the Inland Sea.

The most southern and third largest of the main islands is Kyushu (key-oo-shoe). Beppu is a city of international fame for its hot springs and mineral baths nestled in the serene mountains and plateaus on the eastern shore. There are several thousands of smaller islands in Japan.

About 72 percent of Japan's land is mountainous. Down the very center of the nation lies a slender mountain range called the Japanese Alps. Japan is so mountainous that there is very little habitable land left. Every bit of land is treasured and used wisely. The highest and most significant mountain is Mt. Fuji (12,388 feet [3716.4 m]).

There are numerous swift rivers, excellent harbors, splendid lakes, sandy beaches, jagged cliffs, peaceful coves, cascading waterfalls and picturesque valleys all over Japan.

Lake Biwa is Japan's largest lake. It is 260 square miles (673.4 sq. km) in size. Several little islands dot its surface and the scenery around the lake is superb.

Japan is surrounded by the Sea of Japan on the west, the Pacific Ocean on the east, the sea of Okhotsk in the north and the Inland Sea on the western side of Shikoku.

There are many semi-active volcanoes due to the fact that Japan is located on the Pacific Ring of Fire. Earthquakes happen on a daily basis. Over the years, many earthquakes have destroyed important cities in Japan. The people are now well-informed about earthquake preparedness.

QUESTIONS:
1. Research the Pacific Ring of Fire. What is it?
2. Which island would you like to visit, and why does it seem intriguing to you?

Copyright © 1992, Good Apple

GA1418

Japanese Geography

Maps can be a great way to get to know a country. Try the following activity and find out about Japan for yourself.

MATERIALS:
    atlases
    encyclopedias
    map pencils
    pencils

ACTIVITY:

Draw some large maps of Japan on your own or use copies of the one with this lesson to make up some different types of maps.

You may choose ideas from these or make up your own:

Political	Places of Interest
Population	Flora and Fauna (plants and animals)
Industries	Temperatures and Precipitation
Products	Surrounding Nations
Festivals	Prefectures (like our states)
Ocean Currents	Physical Features
Shrines	Historical Events

1. Make a map of your own country. Make a map of Japan or use the one with this lesson. Compare your country with Japan by making maps of one or more of the topics listed.

2. Label the maps in all capital letters. Outline the maps and all labels with a fine line black marker.

3. Color the maps lightly with map pencils.

4. Look carefully at the two maps and write three similarities and three differences about them. If you wish, you may use the "Similarities and Differences" page for this.

5. Draw some conclusions about the findings on your maps.

Copyright © 1992, Good Apple GA1418

Japanese Geography

Map Title _____   Name _____

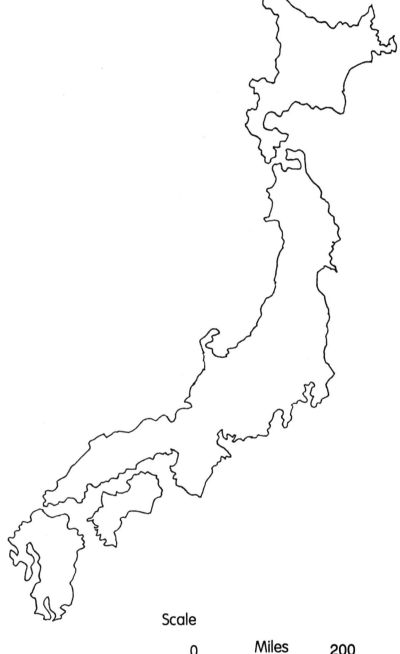

Map Legend

Scale

Miles

0   200

Copyright © 1992, Good Apple

7

GA1418

Similarities and Differences

Topic

Japan

United States

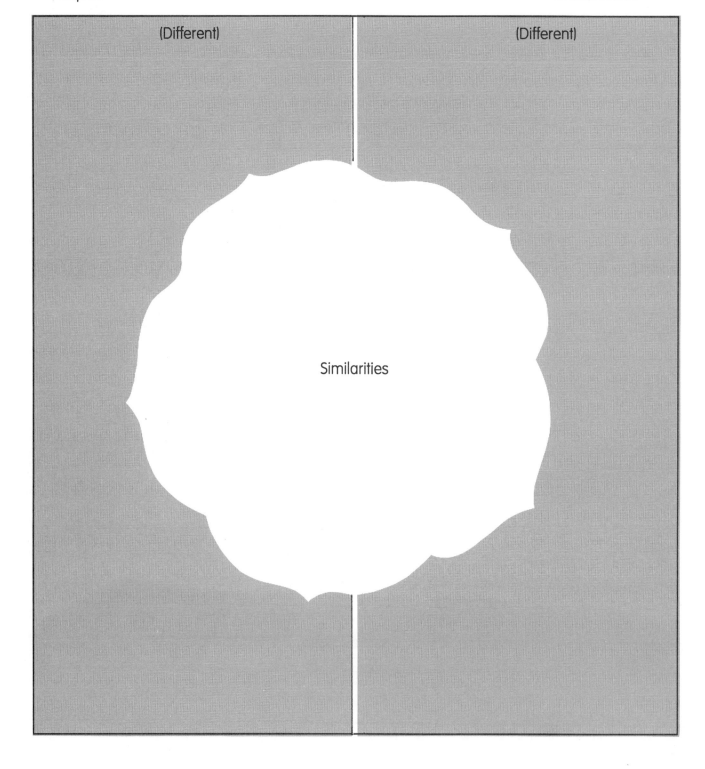

(Different)

(Different)

Similarities

Copyright © 1992, Good Apple

GA1418

Fun and Games in Japan

In many ways Japanese people have fun the same way we do. These are but a few of the ways the Japanese enjoy themselves.

People love to go on picnics on their days off. They also enjoy visiting lakes for water skiing, swimming, boating, and fishing.

Track, field events, and jogging are popular. Modern sports include basketball, Ping-Pong, soccer, golf, volleyball, tennis, swimming, biking, skating and ice hockey. Children love to play games. Baseball is the most popular modern sport in the country. High schools have championships that everyone watches. Little league, company and professional baseball teams can be found all over Japan. Baseball is serious business there.

Many Japanese like to go to the movies, bookstores, record and toy shops. Meals are often eaten while watching TV. You will find out that most Japanese people love to sing and dance. The karaoke singing machine has been popular there for several years. People sing along with recorded band music in nightclubs, on buses, in taxicabs, and just about anywhere. Don't be surprised if they hand you a microphone, too.

Traditional Japanese recreational activities are taught during after-school clubs. These include the ever-popular and ancient sumo wrestling matches. Kendo is fencing with bamboo poles. Karate and judo are also popular sports.

It is common to visit the Grand Kabuki Theatre to see ancient plays with colorful costumes, elaborate makeup and starring an all-male cast. Children love bunraku (bun-rack-coo). These are plays written long ago and are staged with almost life-size puppets. Dramatic masks are worn by Noh theatre actors as they perform historical plays passed down over the years

Girls and boys both collect and display dolls on Children's Day, May 5th. These are never played with but are treasured and handed down from parent to child. Girls' dolls, displayed on Girl's Day, March 3, represent the Emperor and Empress and lords and ladies of the imperial court. Boys collect samurai swords and warrior dolls.

Kite flying is a traditional pastime for old and young. Origami, or paper folding, is another activity handed down from one generation to the next. Many people practice the art of ikebana (ik-key-bah-nah) which is Japanese flower arranging. A relaxing afternoon might be spent enjoying the tea ceremony.

The Japanese delight in painting with watercolors, carving, sculpting, and doing brush painting, called calligraphy.

Copyright © 1992, Good Apple

GA1418

Fun and Games in Japan

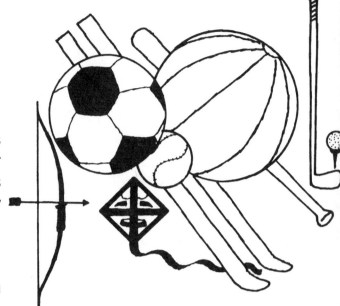

QUESTIONS:

What type of things do we, as Americans, pass from one generation to the next? Describe your own family traditions that you would like to pass on to your children. Give a reason for each. Why do you think people do this?

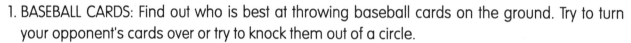

ACTIVITY:

These games were observed while visiting a Japanese school. Try some.

1. BASEBALL CARDS: Find out who is best at throwing baseball cards on the ground. Try to turn your opponent's cards over or try to knock them out of a circle.

2. HOBBLE RACE: Line up two teams, one behind the other along a starting line. Place a turn around line some distance away. Tie a bow around the knees of the first person in each line. At a given signal, both players quickly hobble up to and cross over the turn around line. They remove the cloth and run full speed back to the next person in line. Each person must tie his/her own bow. The first team to finish all players, wins.

3. FUNNEL RACE: Make a long funnel-like snout to tie around the heads of two or more players (use poster board and scarves). The hole at the bottom is about the size of a silver dollar and the other is the size of the face. The player should not be able to see out the sides. Attach one scarf or tie on each side of the hole where the face will go. Form any number of teams of equal size. Have a starting and turn around line. You will need a kickball. Tie the funnels, in a bow, on the heads of the first students in line. On the signal, the first person on each team dribbles the ball over the turn around line, removes the funnel and races back. Each player must tie the funnel, in a bow, by himself. Repeat for all team players. First team finished, wins. This game is hilarious.

Copyright © 1992, Good Apple

GA1418

Yakko Kites

One of the traditional Japanese handicrafts is making miniature Yakko kites. These tiny kites are flown for good luck. In the old days, Hideoyoshi started his life as a Yakko or footman on a farm. He finally ended up attaining the rank of Premier, the highest rank accessible to subjects of the land. In Japan boys fly Yakko kites, wishing to be as successful as Hideoyoshi.

MATERIALS:
  1 thin piece of bamboo 6 $\frac{3}{4}$" x $\frac{1}{4}$" (17.14 x 6 cm) (horizontal piece)
  1 thin piece of bamboo 5 $\frac{3}{4}$" x $\frac{1}{4}$" (14.6 x 6 cm) (vertical piece)
  paper for kite shape
  glue
  paper tail $\frac{3}{4}$" x 21" (1.9 x 53.34 cm)
  3 yards (2.73 m) of very thin kite string
  small label $\frac{1}{2}$" x 1" (1.25 x 2.54 cm)

ACTIVITY:
  You will make a Yakko kite and have a kite flying contest to see whose kite flies the highest, longest, quickest up, most maneuverable.
  1. Make and color in bright colors, your own pattern from the kite on this page (about 4" [10.16 cm] from top to bottom).
  2. Glue the horizontal bamboo across the wing on the blank side, extending just beyond the edge on both sides.
  3. Glue the vertical piece of bamboo down the center on the blank side. You may need to cut a little v-shape in the bamboo for it to fit.
  4. When thoroughly dry, wrap kite string around bamboo wing pieces a few times each and tie a knot. Cut the leftover string.
  5. Wrap the long kite string that will pass through the hole, around the center of the horizontal string and tie a knot.
  6. From the blank side, use a pin to pass the leftover string up through the center of the front. Before pulling it all the way to the inside, make a thick knot on the end. This knot will remain on the blank side so this string won't pass through the hole.

  7. To prevent the paper from tearing, put the label over the hole.
  8. Glue the tail on.
  9. Learn the song "Let's Go Fly a Kite" and sing it at the contest.

Copyright © 1992, Good Apple   GA1418

President or Emperor?

ACTIVITY:

Research information on the powers, duties, advantages, and disadvantages of both President of the United States and the Emperor of Japan. Take notes as you read by writing down key words in the appropriate boxes below. When you have completed the boxes, answer the question at the bottom of the page.

President of the United States

Advantages	Powers	Duties	Disadvantages

Emperor of Japan

Advantages	Powers	Duties	Disadvantages

QUESTION:

After filling out the boxes with key words, decide whether you would prefer being the Emperor of Japan or President of the United States and give supporting details for your decision.

Copyright © 1992, Good Apple

GA1418

People Can Be Puzzling

There are many famous Japanese people who did great and important things. Among these is Minamoto no Yoritomo. He was the first Shogun (military leader) of Japan. He introduced the feudal system in 1185.

The Ashikaga shoguns built magnificent palaces and gardens, many of which are now national treasures. The golden age of arts and letters developed during the early part of the fourteenth century.

The most dedicated patron of the arts was Shogun Yoshimasa. He built one of the most gorgeous buildings in Japan, the Silver Pavilion, in Kyoto, in the fifteenth century. He gathered together artists, writers, poets, painters and landscape designers to lay down formal rules for art.

The Tokugawa family ruled Japan beginning in 1603 and ruled it for over 250 years.

Emperor Meiji moved the Imperial Court from Kyoto to Tokyo in 1868. His work helped Japanese life change and improve drastically. This period of growth became known as the "Meiji Restoration."

Emperor Hirohito ascended the throne of Japan in 1926. He died in 1989, after a sixty-three-year reign. Upon the death of his father, Prince Akihito became emperor on January 7, 1989.

Hiroshige was a Japanese artist who was best known for his exquisite wood-block prints.

Confucius was a great philosopher who greatly influenced the Japanese people. He taught them about close family ties, honor and respect for the aged.

ACTIVITIES:

1. Using the facts above, create your own crossword puzzle on the sheet that follows.

2. Next try to create a word search using the names of famous people in Japanese history.

Copyright © 1992, Good Apple

GA1418

People Can Be Puzzling

Across

Down

Copyright © 1992, Good Apple

GA1418

Historical Time Line

The earliest prehistoric inhabitants of Japan were the tribal people called Ainu. They are believed to have lived there from 700 B.C. to 400 A.D. Historians think they may be of Mongol origins.

According to legend, Jimmu, Japan's first Emperor, ascended the throne in 660 A.D. and started the Japanese Empire.

During the fourth century, the powerful Yamato family took over all kingdoms and ruled for several hundreds of years.

From the ninth to the nineteenth centuries, powerful clans ruled Japan. For a period of one thousand years, Japan was ruled by only six different families and two Shoguns (military leaders).

Japan closed its doors to the rest of the world in 1630. Upon the arrival of a United States naval officer, Commodore Matthew Perry in 1853, Japan reopened her doors.

Emperor Meiji ruled Japan from 1867 to 1912. Japan became an industrialized and more modern nation under his reign. Emperor Hirohito followed in his footsteps in 1926.

World War II started in 1939. The United States was concerned with the amount of power Japan was gaining and cut off all exports to Japan. This angered Japan, greatly. Japan bombed military bases at Pearl Harbor in Hawaii, on December 7th, 1941. The United States then dropped the first atomic bomb on Hiroshima, Japan, on August 6th, 1945. Japan surrendered to General Douglas MacArthur on August 14, 1945. From 1945 to 1952 Japan was under United States occupation. A treaty was signed between Japan and the United States in 1952.

Emperor Hirohito died in 1989 after a sixty-three-year reign. His son, Akihito, ascended the throne that same year.

Copyright © 1992, Good Apple

GA1418

Historical Time Line

Put the dates and events in correct order.

Historical Events Taking Place in the United States and Japan

Japan		United States	
1989	Emperor Hirohito dies	1990	Troops enter Saudi Arabia
1867	Emperor Meiji to throne	1607	Jamestown settled
1637	Japan closes doors to outside	1492	Columbus sets sail
1956	Japan joins the United Nations	1941	Pearl Harbor bombed
1989	Akihito ascends throne	1776	Declaration of Independence
1941	Japan attacks Pearl Harbor	1958	First U. S. satellite in orbit
1637	St. Francis Xavier visits	1950	Korean War begins
1598	Tokugawa family in power	1620	Coastal New England settled by Pilgrims
1783	Rice riots start		
1853	Commodore Perry comes to Japan	1789	Washington becomes first President
1889	Constitution adopted and National Diet opened	1969	First manned flight and landing on the moon
1926	Hirohito becomes Emperor	1812	War of 1812
1600	Civil wars end	1945	First atomic bomb dropped in Hiroshima
1972	Winter Olympics in Tokyo		
1952	U.S. occupation of Japan ends	1906	San Francisco earthquake
1894	War with China	1848	Gold discovered in California
1923	Earthquake destroys Tokyo	1861	Civil wars begin
1543	First Europeans reach Japan	1917	World War I begins
1904	Japan becomes world power	1965	U.S. troops in Vietnam
1937	War with China during WW II	1930	Great Depression

ACTIVITIES:

1. Climb aboard the "Bullet Train" and travel back in time. In what era did you stop? Describe what you see. Who is there? What is happening? What do people look like? What are they wearing?

2. What do you predict will happen in Japan in the years ahead?

Copyright © 1992, Good Apple

GA1418

Historical Time Line

Time lines can make it easier for us to understand the history of a country and simplify comparing two countries with each other.

MATERIALS:

a 36" x 8" (91.44 x 20.32 cm) strip of paper for each individual or small group
two different colors of markers
copies of the historical events in Japan and the states
copy of time line frame
scissors

ACTIVITY:

1. Cut out the time line frame.
2. Place the bottom of the 1400's under the 1600's and glue.
3. Place the bottom of this long strip under the top of the 1800's strip and glue it. You should now have one long strip dating from the 1400's to the year 2000.
4. Glue the long thin time line frame strip down the center of the 36" x 8" (91.44 x 20.32 cm) strip.
5. Using one of the markers, list all the historical events for Japan, in their proper order, down the left-hand side.
6. Do the same for the United States down the right-hand side.

QUESTIONS:

1. What major events were taking place, simultaneously?
2. Were there times when either country was making major changes and the other wasn't? What were they?

Copyright © 1992, Good Apple

Historical Time Line

1400

1500

glue

1600

1700

glue

1800

1900

2000

Copyright © 1992, Good Apple

GA1418

Tomatoes for Toyotas

Many products are traded between Japan and the United States. Students will survey certain products in their homes to find out where they came from. Next they will form cooperative learning teams to combine their surveys. As a group they will create bar graphs for each product and country. They then will draw some conclusions regarding who our most common trading partners are and what types of products we are trading.

MATERIALS:
    copies of the Family Survey (one per child, one per team)
    copies of the Bar Graph Sheet (three for each team)
    colored markers
    pencils

ACTIVITY:
1. Students will fill out their Family Surveys for homework.
2. Form groups of three to four students and have them combine their tallies on the extra Family Survey sheet.
3. Next take the Bar Graph Sheet, number the first chart #1 and list the product name, television.
4. Using the team Family Survey sheet for the total, find the U.S.A. column on the bar graph sheet and place a dot on the space opposite the total number of television sets for the team.
5. Place a dot on the line opposite the total number of television sets for Japan.
6. Continue following this same pattern for all countries and all products.
7. Using a different color marker for each country, and using that same color for the same country on every chart, color in the bar graphs.
8. Examine each chart and draw two conclusions about it. Think about who the United States trades with the least or the most, for instance.
9. When all the teams have completed their surveys, try repeating the same activity as an entire class.

Copyright © 1992, Good Apple

GA1418

Tomatoes for Toyotas

Family Survey

	U.S.A.	JAPAN	TAIWAN	KOREA	OTHER
TELEVISION					
RADIO					
CAMERA					
WATCH					
STEREO					
CAR					
COMPUTER					
MOTORCYCLE					
BICYCLE					

Family Name _____   Team Number _____

Copyright © 1992, Good Apple

GA1418

Tomatoes for Toyotas
Bar Graph Sheet

Chart # _____

Product _____

Over 12					
11					
10					
9					
8					
7					
6					
5					
4					
3					
2					
1					
0					
	U.S.A.	Japan	Taiwan	Korea	Other

Conclusions:

Chart # _____

Product _____

Over 12					
11					
10					
9					
8					
7					
6					
5					
4					
3					
2					
1					
0					
	U.S.A.	Japan	Taiwan	Korea	Other

Conclusions:

Chart # _____

Product _____

Over 12					
11					
10					
9					
8					
7					
6					
5					
4					
3					
2					
1					
0					
	U.S.A.	Japan	Taiwan	Korea	Other

Conclusions:

Chart # _____

Product _____

Over 12					
11					
10					
9					
8					
7					
6					
5					
4					
3					
2					
1					
0					
	U.S.A.	Japan	Taiwan	Korea	Other

Conclusions:

Copyright © 1992. Good Apple

GA1418

Charting the Weather

You will find that the weather in Japan is as varied as ours. In the northern islands of Japan the weather ranges from cool to freezing, and it snows in the winter. The climate is subtropical in the southern islands near Kyushu. Generally speaking, summers in Japan are hot and humid while the winters can be icy cold.

You can experience four distinct seasons on the main island of Honshu. The rainy season occurs during the spring and summer months. This is the monsoon season. You can feel the typhoon season coming at the end of summer because it is sticky and quite hot. Typhoons are major storms that often cause massive destruction and damage.

Just about every kind of weather that exists can be experienced in Japan. It just depends upon where you are.

QUESTIONS:
1. What kinds of special problems would typhoons and monsoons bring to the people of Japan?
2. What kinds of natural disasters do you experience in your area?
3. How do you prepare for them?
4. What kinds of damage do they do?
5. Make a list of suggestions to send to the mayor of your city about how people can be better prepared for disasters in your community?

ACTIVITY:
1. Find out where you can find the daily temperatures for Tokyo and the major city nearest your city.
2. Design a chart for yourself, similar but larger, as shown.
3. Chart temperatures daily for Tokyo and the major city nearest you for one week.
4. Average the temperatures for the week.
5. As individuals, partners, and as an entire class, draw five conclusions about the weather in both cities for the week.

Example:

WEATHER CHART

	Mon.	Tues.	Wed.	Thurs.	Fri.
Tokyo					
Your City					
Conclusions					

Copyright © 1992, Good Apple

GA1418

To Be or Not to Be?

On December 7th, 1941, the Japanese attacked the United States military bases in Pearl Harbor, Hawaii. The United States Naval fleet was all but obliterated. In retaliation, the United States

dropped an atomic bomb Japan, on August 6, 1945. troyed and over 200,000 9th, the United States drop-on the city of Nagasaki, were directly related to the

on the city of Hiroshima, Most of the city was des-people were killed. On August ped an even larger bomb Japan. These two events ending of World War II.

Today several nations have powerful and terrifying nuclear bombs. Some people believe that in order to help keep the world safe, all nuclear bombs should be destroyed and there should be no more made. Others feel we need these bombs to protect ourselves against terrorists and other nations who might choose to use them on us.

ACTIVITY:

A debate titled "To Be or Not to Be?"

1. The teacher will be the moderator.
2. Divide the students into pro and con teams.
3. Elect a group leader, spokesperson and recorder.
4. The question: "Should the United States have nuclear bombs?"
5. Groups should brainstorm reasons for their position. Notes should be written on the debate form by each student during brainstorming sessions. They may refer to the debate form throughtout the debate.
6. In order to be ready for the rebuttal, brainstorm the other team's possible responses and come up with some responses of your own.
7. Set up the rules for the debate.
8. Run the debate. Notes can be added to the debate form. The debate sheet can be used to assist them with their personal decision.
9. At the end of the debate, students will vote secretly on the question and give three reasons for their choice.
10. Tell the results of the vote. Draw conclusions about the results.
11. Remind students that there are no totally right or wrong opinions.

VARIATIONS:

"President vs. Emperor" or "U.S. vs. Japanese Education"

Copyright © 1992, Good Apple

GA1418

To Be or Not to Be?

Debate Form

Date _____ Name_____

Use for brainstorming, note-taking, debate and final decision.

Debate question_____ Pro or con? _____

Pro Arguments   Con Arguments

Your final decision: (yes or no)_____

Reason 1 _____
_____

Reason 2 _____
_____

Reason 3 _____
_____

Copyright © 1992, Good Apple

GA1418

Temple Books and Language

Most people in Japan follow both the Buddhist and Shinto religions. Each time they visit a shrine they bring a Temple Book, and the priests add a beautiful bit of calligraphy on one of the pages in the little book.

Ideographs came from China about 2000 years ago. These symbols represent both a specific meaning and at least one sound.

The first written Japanese language is called Hiragana. It is learned even before students enter kindergarten. Language is written in columns from the right to the left and from top to bottom.

It is quite easy to learn how to speak Japanese. Purchase a Japanese language tape and become an expert.

The word for **Japan** is **Nippon** which means "land of the rising sun," and it is written....

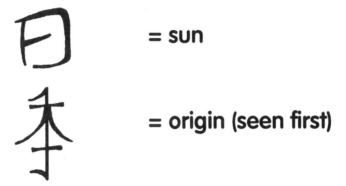

= sun

= origin (seen first)

QUESTIONS:
1. Why do you think people in our country should learn to speak Japanese?
2. Why do you think people in Japan should learn to speak English?
3. Do you think the Japanese would respond in the same way you did? Why do you think so?

THE END | DOUGH-SO PLEASE | EE-YAH NO | MAH-TAH-NAY SEE YOU AGAIN | CON-BAN WAH GOOD EVENING | GUY-GIN TOURIST | TEMPLE BOOK

ACTIVITY 1:
1. Make an accordion book (Temple Book) and on each page write a Japanese phrase or word and its translation. (See phrases on next page.)

2. Memorize some of the phrases and converse with a friend. Fill in with English when you don't have a Japanese word or phrase.

3. Write this dialogue down in story form for practice using proper quotation marks. Share your story with two friends.

Copyright © 1992. Good Apple

GA1418

Temple Books and Language

ACTIVITY 2:

Using the pronunciation guide and the pronunciation spellings, see if you can figure out the proper Japanese spellings for the words or phrases below.

There are five standard vowel sounds:

a = as in father
e = as in red
i = as in piano
o = as in cord
u = as in flute

Word or Phrase	Pronunciation
Good morning.	oh-hi-yo-go-zai-mus
Good afternoon.	co-knee-chee-wah
Good evening.	con-bon-wah
Please.	dough-zo
Thank you.	ah-ree-gah-toe-go-zai-mus
Yes.	high (spoken quickly)
No.	ee-yah
Excuse me.	go-men-coo-dah-sigh
How are you?	go-key-gen-ee-kah-dess-kah
I'm fine, thank you.	ah-ree-gah-toe, gen-key-dess
I am pleased to meet you.	oh-men-nay-kah-kah-ret-tay oo-ray-she-de(ss)
I have appreciated your hospitality.	oh-mow-ten-ah-she-ah-ree-gah-toe-go-zai-musht(a)
See you again.	mah-tahn-nay
tourist	guy-gin
Japan	knee-pohn
Good-bye.	sigh-oh-nah-rah

Copyright © 1992, Good Apple

26

GA1418

Sadako and the Thousand Paper Cranes

A book by Eleanor Coerr*

This is a marvelous story about a ten-year-old leukemia victim from Japan. The activity of story-telling and retelling leads to greater understanding of what they have read. It is important for the children to understand this. They are not to memorize all the facts of the story but rather they should just try to understand the story as a whole. Run this activity in a very nonthreatening manner.

ACTIVITY 1:

1. Before reading the book aloud, divide the class into groups of four (even number in each group, two is better than six).
2. Based on the title, children will write down two predictions as to what they think this story is about. (1 minute)
3. They can assume their predictions are correct. Next, they will predict some vocabulary words or phrases they feel they will come in contact with when they read the story. (1 minute)
4. Within their small groups, each student discusses one of his predictions about the title or the vocabulary and phrases and the reason for his prediction. (5 minutes)
5. The teacher reads the story aloud. Remind students it is important to understand the story, not to memorize it.
6. Have the students write their retelling of the story. (10 minutes)
7. Meet in pairs and share the written retelling of the story.
   a. Pairs read and discuss if anything was added to or left out of either story. Give a reason for each.
   b. Switch partners and do the same thing again.
8. As a class, share some of the retellings.
9. They should know the story fairly well by now.
10. As a class, discuss the ways Sadako showed courage.
11. Share the meanings of **leukemia, radiation** and **atomic bombs**.
12. Why was the statue of Sadako built?
13. What were some of the tender moments in the story?
14. What prompted the bombing? Was it the right decision?
15. What did we hope to achieve by dropping the bomb?

*Sadako and the Thousand Paper Cranes** by Eleanor Coerr, Del Publications, 1977. Further Reading: **Crow Boy** and **the Big Wave**.

Copyright © 1992, Good Apple

GA1418

Sadako and the Thousand Paper Cranes

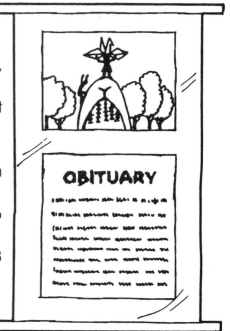

ACTIVITY 2:

1. Look up the word **obituary**.
2. Find some obituaries in the newspaper to share.
3. Discuss their purposes.
4. Find some information on Peace Park located in Hiroshima, Japan, if possible. Is there a picture of Sadako's statue?
5. If a picture is unavailable, discuss what a monument might look like.
6. Write an obituary for Sadako. (Do a rough draft.)
7. Design a new monument to honor Sadako and the children who died. (Do a rough draft.)
8. Cut a piece of green construction paper (8" x 14" [20.32 x 35.56 cm]).
9. Cut a piece of white construction paper (6" x 12" [15.24 x 30.48 cm]).
10. Draw the monument on the top half of the white paper.
11. Write the obituary on the bottom half.
12. Color the monument and the area around it.
13. Glue the white paper on the green.
14. Share the obituaries in small groups and give a reason for each item on the monument.

ACTIVITY 3:

Invite a Japanese friend to class to teach the students how to fold the paper cranes.

ACTIVITY 4:

Make 1000 paper cranes and send them to the mayor of Hiroshima, Japan. Ask him to have them placed at Sadako's monument in Peace Park. Hint: Keep the cranes folded for mailing and string them one under the other.

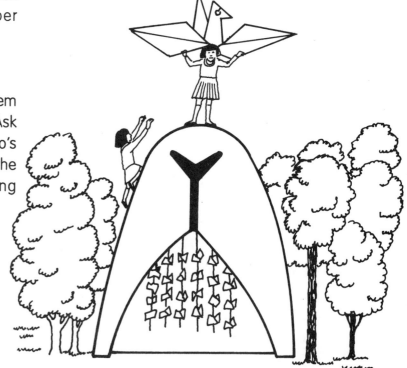

Copyright © 1992, Good Apple

28

Transportation on Parade

The main and most important method of transportation in Japan is the train. There are commuter trains that make several stops along the way, picking up people in the suburbs and rural areas, as they make their way to and from work. Commuter trains are so crowded during the rush hour that there are actually people called pushers who literally push people into the trains so that more people are able to fit inside. It is so unbelievably crowded that if you rise up on your tiptoes you cannot come back down again until someone else leaves the train. Subway trains move at a very fast pace. One comes every two minutes and you have only sixty seconds to enter and exit the trains.

The trains that travel farther distances are called bullet trains. They are among the fastest trains in the world. The extensive network of trains, some 17,000 miles of railways, can bring you from one end of an island to the other. Many of the trains run underground. The bullet trains are spacious, neat and clean. Delicious boxed lunches called obento can be purchased on board as sellers move up and down the aisles.

Cars are popular in Japan. In order to purchase a car, though, you must prove you have a parking space for it. Traffic is hectic in the cities and the cost of owning and maintaining an automobile is quite high. It is for these three reasons that many people do not own cars. The train system is so extensive and efficient that a car isn't really necessary.

Trucks move most of the goods on busy freeways. People also ride buses, bikes, motorcycles, scooters and taxicabs. Since Japan is a major crossroad for the world, the main airport at Narita is often busy and crowded.

Japan is the world's leading ship builder and constructs about half of the world's tonnage. Many things are imported and exported by ship. Smaller boats and hydrofoils take people from island to island.

QUESTION:
    As you can see, the commuter trains are unbelievably crowded during rush hours. Describe one or more ways that the Japanese might solve this serious problem.

ACTIVITY:
    Create a miniature "rose parade" type float using a shoe box. Put different types of transportation on it. Label each one. Use the box cover for the back of the float. Explain the things on the float and give some background information about each to the class.

Copyright © 1992, Good Apple

GA1418

Using Japanese Numbers

English	Japanese	Sound Spelling	Written
ONE	ICHI	EE-CHEE	一
TWO	NI	KNEE	二
THREE	SAN	SAHN	三
FOUR	SHI	SHE	四
FIV E	GO	GO	五
SIX	ROKU	ROW-COO	六
SEVEN	SHICHI	SHE-CHEE	七
EIGHT	HACHI	HA-CHEE	几
NINE	KU	COO	九
TEN	JU or JUU	JEW	十
ZERO	ZERO	ZEE-ROW	〇

SAMPLE: 10 + 6 = 16   16 = JU + ROKU = JU ROKU   十六

Answer these questions writing both Japanese numbers and words.

1. What is your phone number?_____

2. How old are you?_____

3. What is your ZIP code? _____

Copyright © 1992, Good Apple

GA1418

Using Japanese Numbers

ACTIVITY:

Using a pointed paintbrush and black paint, practice making your numbers several times. When you have finished, do the math page for this lesson.

1	6
2	7
3	8
4	9
5	10

Copyright © 1992. Good Apple

Using Japanese Numbers

Arabic		Japanese		Arabic		Japanese
1	〜	ICHI		6	六	ROKU
2	二	NI		7	七	SHICHI
3	三	SAN		8	八	HACHI
4	四	SHI		9	九	KU
5	五	GO		10	十	JU

Translate the Japanese numbers into Arabic and write them. Solve the problems in Arabic only.

Addition

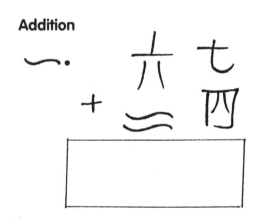

Subtraction

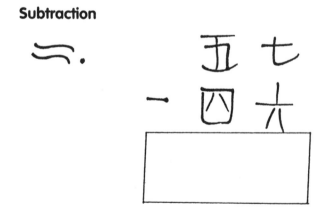

Multiplication

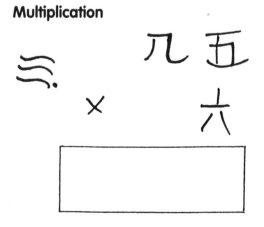

Division

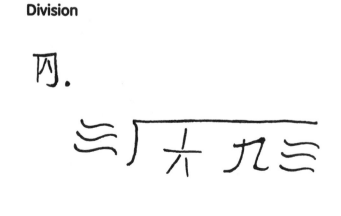

Copyright © 1992, Good Apple

32

GA1418

A Yen to Spend

Japan's economy used to be based solely on the fishing and farming industries. Now less than 10 percent of the people are farmers. There is little land left for farming and newer industries have taken over. Fishing is still important to this island nation, but more and more people are flocking to the cities for jobs in the business world.

Today rice is still the staple in their diet, and it is eaten at almost every meal. The farmer of today also may grow barley, wheat, rye, sweet potatoes, soybeans, potatoes, red beans, peanuts, carrots, cucumbers, eggplant, radishes, onions, cabbage, spinach, tea and tobacco. Grazing land is limited. Farmers raise hogs, some cattle, a few horses, chickens, goats and silkworms.

Popular fruits grown include apples, mandarin oranges, persimmons, oranges, plums, grapes, peaches and strawberries.

The average person consumes over 55 pounds (24.75 kg) of fish per year. The Japanese people cannot catch enough fish for their whole nation and therefore must import some to meet their needs. Some of the fish they catch and enjoy are flounder, pike, cod, mackerel, sardines, tuna, salmon, shrimp, lobster, crab, whale, scallops, bonita, squid, mussels, oysters and clams. Cultured pearls come from special oysters that are not eaten.

Iron and steel industries are of major importance to Japan's economy. Cars, TV sets, VCR's, shipbuilding, electrical machinery, cameras, large appliances, office equipment, radios, watches and stereos are all made there. They also make dinnerware, chemicals and textiles. Robots are used extensively in factories.

People work eight hours a day, six days a week. They are very loyal to their companies. Often a son or daughter will work for the same company as his or her father, and the father may stay with the same company until his retirement.

QUESTIONS:

1. What are several advantages and disadvantages for using robots in factories?

2. List several types of jobs which should never be replaced by robots and give a reason for each.

3. Over the years, how have jobs changed in your country? Why have these changes taken place?

Copyright © 1992. Good Apple

GA1418

A Yen to Spend

You are going on a souvenir hunt and shopping spree in the Ginza, one of Tokyo's most well-known and busiest shopping areas. Have fun!

ACTIVITY:

You will need to find out the value of the Japanese yen. Where might you find this information?

$1.00 USA = _____ yen

Gina Souvenir Center

ichiban T-shirt = Y800   kimono = Y2800   happi coat = Y250

1 pair of geta = Y500   1 pair of chopsticks = Y250

1 set of Kabuki Theatre tickets = Y1000   Dinner for 2 = Y2500

1 fan = Y285   1 rice bowl = Y225   1 cricket cage = Y125

Chie has 1100 yen to spend. List three things she could buy.

Item	Cost
1. _____	Y _____
2. _____	Y _____
3. _____	Y _____ Total = Y_____

Is there any change? _____ If so, how much? Y _____

Copyright © 1992, Good Apple

34

GA1418

A Yen to Spend

2. How much yen does Setsu have if she has $ 9.00 in American money?

    Y_____

3. Your parents gave you 5000 yen to spend. Have a blast and try to spend it all.

Items	Cost
_____	Y _____
_____	Y _____
_____	Y _____
_____	Y _____
_____	Y _____
_____	Y _____
_____	Y _____
	TOTAL=Y5000

4. Hirohito has 2000 yen. He bought one pair of chopsticks and one ichiban T-shirt.
    a. How much did he spend? Y_____
    b. How much change in yen did he receive? Y_____

5. Ten children went to see the exciting Kabuki Theatre. In yen, how much was spent on tickets?
    Y_____

6. Megumi, Kimiko, and Momo want to share the cost of a kimono with you. How much will each person pay?   Y_____

7. How many yen do you need to buy a dinner for twelve, a fan, and a cricket cage? Y_____

8. Your mother said you could buy one of every single item, set, or pair.

    a. How much would you need all together?   Y_____

    b. How much is that in American dollars ? $_____

    c. What would be the amount of yen left over?   Y_____

9. Make up your own problem. Make sure it is a two-step problem.

10. Make up your own problem. Make sure it is a three-step problem.

EXTENSION:
    One week from today check the value of the yen. Did it go up or down? How could this affect

Copyright © 1992, Good Apple   GA1418

Friendship T-Shirt

ACTIVITY:

Design a new T-shirt that illustrates the friendship between the United States and Japan. Keep in mind all the ways we work together and all the ways we are similar. Think about what is going on now and what you think we might be sharing in the future. Decorate the front and the back. Paint or draw your design on a real T-shirt.

QUESTION:

What does each symbol or word on your T-shirt represent or mean, and why did you select it?

Copyright © 1992, Good Apple

GA1418

School Days, School Days

FACTS ABOUT JAPANESE SCHOOLS:

1. Students study the same basic subjects: math, science, citizenship, music, physical education, reading, social studies, art.
2. There are after-school clubs where they learn karate, flower arranging, kendo, and calligraphy.
3. They also go to school for half a day on Saturdays.
4. Difficult exams are taken to get into the best schools.
5. Education is the single most important activity for all students.
6. Teachers are among the most admired people in the community.
7. There is a massive amount of pressure to get good grades at all levels.
8. Japanese is taught early on and English starts in junior high.
9. Students clean inside the school and out, each day.
10. Shoes are not worn in the school. Tennis shoes or slippers are.
11. Older students wear uniforms.
12. They eat lunch with their teacher in the classroom.
13. Most of their science is hands-on.
14. Some students have to go to after-school school just to keep up.
15. Students and teachers bow to each other in the morning.
16. It is important to the whole family for a student to get good grades in school in order to attend the best junior-senior high school and college and get the best job available.
17. Daily homework lasts three to four hours.

QUESTIONS:

1. What are the main differences between schools in Japan and schools in the United States?
2. Find positive things about Japan's schools that we do not have and write a letter to the United States Secretary of Education and make some recommendations for improvements in our system.

ACTIVITY:

1. Start an after-school club (tennis, games, drama).
2. Set up the rules and regulations.
3. Collect dues and give them to a charitable organization such as a shelter for the homeless.

Copyright © 1992, Good Apple

GA1418

Growing the Noble Iris

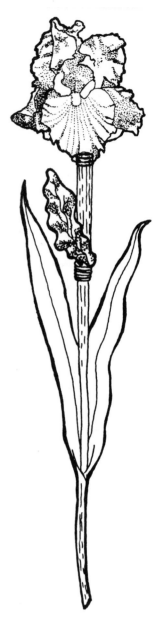

The iris is a much-loved flower of the Japanese people. It is believed to have the power to ward off evil spirits. It can also be found in homes to scare away illness and epidemics.

Leaves are stuffed into sleeping pillows of boys for good health. Drinks are made out of irises and are given to sons so that they might acquire the spirits of brave warriors.

May is the month of the Iris Festival. The tall stemmed iris is a symbolic flower. Its narrow leaves resemble the sharp blade of the sword, and for many centuries it has been the custom to place iris leaves in a boy's bath to give him martial strength.

MATERIALS:

    one 4" (10.16 cm) plastic flowerpot
    potting soil
    one blue ribbon iris bulb
    bonemeal for plant food (to be used later)

ACTIVITY:

1. Fill the pot with potting soil ($^3/_4$ full).
2. Make a hole with a pencil and place the bulb down about $^3/_4$" (1.9 cm) from the top of the soil (pointed end closest to the top).
3. Keep moist until it sprouts.
4. Once it sprouts, give it a little more water than before. Test for dampness by putting your finger in the soil.
5. Put the pot out in the sunshine each day.
6. Feed the bulb with bonemeal once a week.
7. With the point out of the soil, transplant the iris bulbs that are sprouting into a large pot or in the garden.
8. After it blooms, present it as a gift on Mother's Day.

Copyright © 1992, Good Apple

GA1418

Flowers, Feathers and Fur

The plants, trees, birds, and animals of Japan are highly prized and treasured. Beauty is seen in the smallest and grandest of all living things.

ACTIVITY:

Design bingo cards, markers, and cards for the caller for a bingo game using the plants, animals and birds of Japan.

1. Divide the class into three teams (1 for flowers and trees; 1 for animals, pets, reptiles, and insects; and 1 for birds).
2. Each team will find as many species for their topic as they can.
3. Elect a team leader and assign jobs to make the game.
4. As a team, think about the theme and design for each card and marker.
5. Make a calling card for each species (2" x 3" [5.08 x 7.62 cm]).
6. Make the bingo cards (6" x 8" [15.24 x 20.32 cm]).
7. Make markers out of tiny pieces of paper or buttons.
8. Draw a flower, animal or bird in the "free" space.
9. Call the game something other than Bingo. Flora or Fauna, for instance.
10. Try it out with your team.
11. If it works, color and laminate the bingo cards.

VARIATION 1:

1. Make one gigantic game card for birds, one for animals, and one for plants out of a massive piece of paper (about 10' x 12' [3.04 x 3.65 cm]).
2. Follow the directions above for making the games but instead of making markers, use students as living markers for the cards. They will physically walk across the cards.
3. Discuss with the class who should be chosen for a living marker and how.

VARIATION 2:

After researching the plants, animals, and birds of Japan, go outside and make giant bingo cards on the blacktop with chalk. Use the students as living markers. Everyone can help do the research and make the calling cards.

Copyright © 1992, Good Apple

GA1418

Flowers, Feathers and Fur

F	L	O	R	A
lotus	bluebell	peony	azalea	iris
tulip	orchid	rose	cedar	bamboo
pine	violet	FREE	fir	daffodil
willow	beech	spruce	camellia	hollyhock
mulberry	lily	cherry	peach	poppy

TEACHER REFERENCE: If students cannot find names in their research, above are some suggestions. They can just mix them up on the cards.

BIRDS: Geese, hawks, quail, cranes, ducks, eagles, pheasant, plover gulls, cormorants, swan, stork, heron, crane, crown starling, owl, whippoorwill, swallow, nightingale, cuckoo, woodpecker, lark, bobolink, wren, sparrow, ptarmigan, finch, thrush, pelican, vulture, grouse

ANIMALS: Wild boar, wolf, raccoon, weasel, badger, mink, hare, otter, seal, rabbits, rats, bear, black bear, wild dog, monkey, deer, squirrel, fox, and goat antelope. There are not too many wild animals in Japan so the students may include reptiles; insects; and pets such as dogs, cats, fireflies, crickets, grasshoppers, butterflies, dragonflies, bees, cicadas, mosquitos, gnats, Japanese salamanders, chickens, cows, horses, goats, parrots, hamsters, chipmunks, and goldfish.

FLOWERS AND TREES: Trees include cedar, cypress, fir, beech, willow, chestnut, spruce, maple, oak, pine, bamboo, plum, cherry, peach, mulberry, poplar, willow, and bonsai (dwarf trees cultivated by man). Flowers include cherry blossoms, irises, tulips, violets, chrysanthemums, peonies, camellias, roses, daffodils, poppies, hollyhocks, rose of Sharon, water lilies, orchids, and lotus.

PRIZES: What kinds of prizes would be appropriate for this game? Name several.

Copyright © 1992, Good Apple

GA1418

"Fireflies and Snow"

For a long time white snow and fireflies have been symbols of learning and a good education.

A tale brought to Japan from China tells about a man who wanted very much to be an educated man, but he was so poor he had no light by which to study. It is said that he would sit by the window in summer and read by the light of the fireflies, and in winter his source of light was the moon reflecting on the sparkling white snow piled up against his window.

Here are some new lyrics to an old melody, "Auld Lang Syne." The tune is sung at graduation and at closing time in department stores.

ACTIVITY:

1. Make your own music notation sheet and then copy the notes exactly as they are written on the sheet music.
2. Write poetic lyrics to the song for your school's graduation. Write them under the proper music notes.
3. Ask your principal if you and some of your friends could sing it at graduation time.
4. Practice the melody on a keyboard, add some background instruments, record it on tape, and sing it with some friends at graduation. You, too, can be a star !

Write your new title and lyrics under these words.

Title

I have no wealth to buy some light, to learn from every book,

At night the summer fireflies, give light and take a look.

The winter night is cold and dark, I have no light to glow,

But learn I do, as time goes by, as moon reflects off snow.

Copyright © 1992. Good Apple

GA1418

Fireflies and Snow
Lyrics by Carole Allen

I have no wealth to buy some light, to learn from ev - 'ry book, At night the sum - mer fi - re - flies, give light and take a look.

Refrain

The win - ter night is cold and dark, I have no light to glow, But learn I do, as time goes by, as moon re - flects off snow.

Copyright © 1992, Good Apple

GA1418

Performing Arts of Japan

Japanese musical instruments include the koto which is a 13-stringed instrument that sits on the floor and sounds a little like a harp.

The samisen is a three-string guitar-like instrument with a long neck.

A hollow bamboo flute called a shakuhachi (sha-coo-hah-chee) and drums of various sizes make up the main traditional instruments.

Two types of dancing include Mai which is associated with the Noh Theatre and the Odori which is seen more frequently in Kabuki Theatre.

Kabuki was first performed and enjoyed in the seventeenth century. Men actors play the parts of both men and women in these dance-drama productions. The stories are usually about the common man and his triumph over the upper class. Stage decorations are kept very simple and serene, but the costumes and makeup are elaborate and elegant.

The Noh Theatre actors wear masks. The painted facial expressions identify the characters. Male actors present historical plays that are based on the warrior and samurai classes. Little scenery is used and a pine tree suggests that the scene is outdoors (as they all used to be). Actions are slow and the actors move with much grace and beauty. Noh Theatre is the oldest of Japan's dramatic arts.

Bunraku (bun-rah-coo) is a theatre play with slightly less than life-size puppets. It takes three puppeteers to move one puppet. Stories are told in chants. These plays evolved from ancient religious ceremonies. These three types of traditional plays are the most often performed today.

Most Japanese people love to sing and dance. Every kind of western style music is enjoyed, danced to, composed, and performed. Rock, jazz, top 40, classical, pop, country western, blues, rap, and folk music can be heard all over Japan. Many symphonies, opera, and ballet companies perform to packed houses. Pop stars and rock stars visit there often.

QUESTIONS:

What type of music came from our early years? How has it changed? Why has it changed?

Copyright © 1992, Good Apple

GA1418

Performing Arts of Japan

ACTIVITY 1:

Design and color Noh Theatre masks for each character in the blank masks shown below.

ACTIVITY 2:

Write a short play centering around one or more of the characters you have designed.

ACTIVITY 3:

Cut oval shapes from paper plates. Using construction paper, tissue paper and markers or tempera paint, create the masks you will need for the play in Activity 2. Glue the masks on tongue depressors. Perform your play for a younger class.

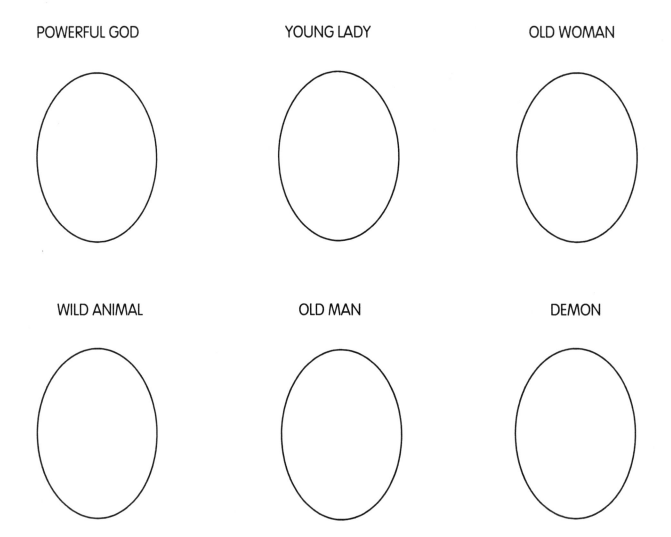

POWERFUL GOD

YOUNG LADY

OLD WOMAN

WILD ANIMAL

OLD MAN

DEMON

Copyright © 1992, Good Apple

GA1418

Painting Hashi
(Chopsticks)

This is a great opportunity to learn how to use chopsticks. Painting chopsticks is challenging because you must paint a design in a very narrow area.

MATERIALS:
   brightly colored tempera paint
   one pair chopsticks for each child
   thin, fine point paintbrushes
   copies of Japanese designs or make up your own

ACTIVITY 1:
1. Make some rough drafts of designs first.
2. Try painting them on the blank chopsticks.

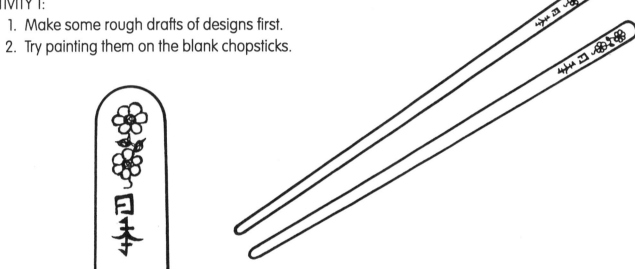

3. Keep the wrapper on the lower half of the chopsticks to keep the eating part of each stick clean.
4. Select your favorite design and paint identical designs on the top of each chopstick. Be careful about not putting paint too close to the part that will go into the mouth.

VARIATIONS:
1. Paint paper plates and cups to match and laminate them.
2. Design a matching place mat.

ACTIVITY 2:
   Have a Japanese obento (boxed) lunch catered and eat it with hashi. Select items that would be enjoyed by most students (not sushi, but salad, tempura shrimp and vegetables, teriyaki chicken or beef and rice). Tell a Japanese restaurant this is educational, and they will probably give you a great price.

Copyright © 1992, Good Apple

GA1418

Fantastic Food Facts

The most outstanding fact about Japanese food is that it is as pleasing to the eye as it is to the stomach. The utmost care is used in arranging the food. The season of the year is very important when selecting the shapes, colors and materials of the dishes being used.

Rice has long been the staple in Japan and still is. A typical meal with rice would include vegetables and boiled or roasted fish or meat, miso soup and pickled vegetables. In addition, there are hors d'oeuvres such as sashimi (raw fish with rice) and sushi. Shellfish are very popular, too. Other well-known dishes include sukiyaki (meat and vegetable dish), yakitori (charbroiled meats) and tempura (vegetables and meats or fish, dipped in batter and deep-fried).

Seasonings include soy sauce, sake (rice wine), vinegar, sugar, horseradish and ginger. All are used sparingly so as not to interfere with the natural flavors of the food.

Dried foods are used to make stock or soups. A few of these foods are dried bonito, shiitake mushrooms and seaweed.

Beef, pork, chicken and seafood of all types are deliciously prepared. Beef is extremely expensive in Japan.

Children learn to eat with chopsticks when they are about three years old. Japanese-style meals are eaten with chopsticks. Other meals are usually eaten with forks.

Children love pizza, hamburgers, spaghetti, fried chicken, hot dogs and soft drinks. Tea is the traditional drink of the Japanese people.

Breakfast is usually quite simple. It can consist of a cup of hot rice, a raw egg that has been broken over the rice and quickly mixed so that the hot rice cooks the egg. This is eaten with bites of seaweed. Bacon, eggs, toast and coffee are also popular.

Obento lunches are special box lunches with a complete meal inside. They are tastefully decorated and contain traditional foods such as rice, vegetables, meat and fish. They come complete with napkins and chopsticks. A ride on the bullet train and a stop at several stations will give you a delectable and varied sampling of the types of Japanese food served across the nation.

Copyright © 1992, Good Apple

GA1418

Fantastic Food Facts Fun

Have some fun! Prepare some of these recipes and share them with your friends.

SALAD (TSUKEMONO) Namasu (Cucumber and Carrot Salad)

Ingredients:
- 1 cucumber
- 4 T. (60 ml) salt
- 1/2 c. (120 ml) of vinegar
- 1 carrot
- 1/4 c. (60 ml) sugar

Peel the cucumber and carrot and slice thinly. Mix salt into sliced vegetables and set aside for 2-3 hours until vegetables are limp. Rinse all the salt off, several times, with water. Mix vinegar and sugar. Add to vegetables. Chill for an hour or more. Serves two.

JAPANESE BREAKFAST

Ingredients:
- 1 c. (240 ml) of hot cooked rice (just cooked)
- 1 egg, scrambled (not yet cooked)
- 1 T. (15 ml) of chopped green onions (optional)
- 2-3 tsp. (10-15 ml) of soy sauce

Put the hot rice in a mug. Pour the egg over the top of the rice and stir quickly so that the rice cooks the egg. Pour in the soy sauce. Sprinkle the green onions on top. Eat with chopsticks. Serves one.

BAR-B-QUE TERIYAKI SAUCE FOR VARIOUS MEATS

Ingredients:
- 3/4 c. (180 ml) soy sauce
- 1 T. (15 ml) sake (wine)
- 1/2 c. (120 ml) of sugar
- 1/2 tsp. (2.5 ml) MSG (optional)
- 1 tsp. (5 ml) grated ginger (fresh)
- 1 clove of garlic (minced)

Cut chicken, spareribs, beef, shrimp or fish into bite-size pieces. Mix all the ingredients together and soak the pieces for at least an hour. Broil over charcoal or under the broiler, as usual, until done.

DESSERTS

| fresh fruit | mandarin oranges | poached pears |
| rice pudding | rice cakes | fruit cocktail |

ACTIVITY:

Use the "Compare and Contrast" sheet and compare the food of Japan with the food in your country. Make a box lunch and eat the food with chopsticks.

Copyright © 1992, Good Apple

GA1418

Compare and Contrast

Topic_____

Japan (Different)	Your Country (Different)

(Same)

Copyright © 1992, Good Apple

GA1418

Japanese Mouse House

Traditional Japanese homes are usually serenely plain and uncluttered. They are made of wood and are often about one or two stories high. The roofs are thatched or made of tile. Often the roofs slant upward as a natural rain drain. From a religious standpoint, the roofs slant upward in order to send evil spirits back into the sky.

The floors are covered with straw mats called tatami. Families and guests always remove their shoes before entering a home. Slippers or two-toed socks called tabi are worn inside. This is necessary in order to keep the mats clean, as they sit and sleep on them.

Many homes, especially those with children, have a more modern kitchen and often have a living room with a TV set. There are areas with tatami mats that have sliding walls to close them off for privacy at bedtime. Bedding is folded up in the morning, walls are moved back and the room again becomes a sitting or dining room.

Furniture is kept to a minimum. Tables are low and people sit on pillows on the floor. The main room has a quiet area called a tokonoma. There an artistic scroll hangs and in front of it sits a low table with a flower arrangement.

Most walls and windows slide sideways to permit the gentle breezes to blow through and allow the family to enjoy the elegant gardens outside which are symbols of paradise.

Bathtubs are different in the traditional home of Japan. They are made of wood and are quite deep. You do not bathe in the actual tub; you soak in it. There is a tiled area beside the tub where there is a showerhead or spigot, a bucket and a small stool. You sit down to soap and rinse yourself outside the tub so you are all clean before entering the relaxing and very hot bath. The father or house guest usually bathes first. The water is not usually changed from person to person. The rooms of modern homes and apartments, on the other hand, are just like ours, only smaller. The Japanese laughingly refer to them as mansions.

QUESTION:

After filling out a "Compare and Contrast" sheet, write a summary of your findings describing the similarities and differences between a traditional Japanese home and an American home at the turn of the century (1890-1900).

Copyright © 1992, Good Apple

GA1418

Japanese Mouse House

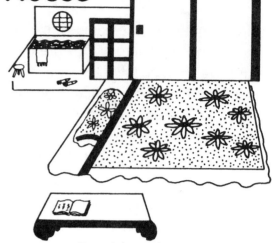

ACTIVITY:

Using what you have learned about the traditional Japanese home, and by further research, create a miniature Japanese home for a family of Japanese mice. You will decorate the home inside and out. Glue everything down so it can be moved from one place to another without falling apart. Make it as authentic as possible.

MATERIALS:

cardboard box with 12"-18" (30.48-45.72 cm) sides
toothpicks
construction paper
small rocks
waxed paper walls
tempera paint
small boxes—bathtub, tables
miniature items

glue
markers
trees
yarn
wall and wrapping paper—Oriental
clay bowls, cups, stand-up items
wood scraps
small flowers

Popsicle sticks
pieces of cardboard
pipe cleaners
small Oriental pictures
1/2 walnut or peanut shell for mice
cloth pillows, bedding, clothes

GETTING STARTED AND HINTS:

1. Box should be sitting on one side, not the bottom, so you can look straight into it, not down into it.
2. Decide what areas you want and where they will be.
3. Do you want one or two stories? Slanted roof?
4. Decorate the outside first, if you are just painting the walls and garden on the sides and back of the box. Lanterns? Carp flying?
5. Decorate the floor with tatami mats. Be creative.
6. Do the walls and decorate them with pictures, scrolls.
7. Put futons (bedding), zabutons (pillows) on floor, mice on them.
8. Make low tables out of small boxes painted black.
9. Make moveable walls (difficult but a good challenge).
10. Use waxed paper for sliding walls and windows.
11. Bathtub with mice in it, towel, slippers, spigot, bucket, stool.
12. TV set, appliances, shoes outside, flower arrangements.
13. Mice eating with toothpick chopsticks, rice in bowls, tea cups.

EXTENSION:

You must have a Japanese home show. Decide which are the most authentic homes, gardens, exteriors, and interiors.

Copyright © 1992. Good Apple

GA1418

Fashions–Then and Now

Adults, teenagers, and younger children in Japan dress just like we do. You rarely see anyone in a kimono out in public unless it is for special occasions such as visits to temples, weddings, funerals, coming of age ceremonies, holidays, receptions, and festivals.

Modern clothing includes items such as jeans, shorts, T-shirts, suits, dresses, slacks, skirts, blouses, sandals, tennis shoes, and shirts. Fashion-conscious Japanese seek out the very hottest fashions from Italy, France, and the U.S.

Traditional Japanese dress for ladies includes an elaborate, long, robe-like dress called a kimono. The more valuable ones are made of brightly colored embroidered silk and may have a slight train in the back. A wide belt worn around the middle and tied at the back is called an obi (oh-bee). Both men and women wear two-toed socks called tabi (tab-ee) which are worn with geta (gay-tah). These are thong-like sandals that are raised up on small platforms. Zoriis are flat sandals made of woven straw and may be worn instead of geta. Women may often wear thick black wigs and bright hair ornaments that dangle. Ladies sometimes carry a fan or a parasol.

The traditional dress for men includes a skirt-like garment with pleats called a hakama (hah-kah-ma). It is usually dark brown or some other dark color. That is worn over a dark kimono. Over all of that is worn a short black or navy kimono-like open jacket called a haori (hah-oh-ri).

Men and women enjoy wearing a yukata (you-kah-tah) which is a cotton kimono that is worn at home and during the summer.

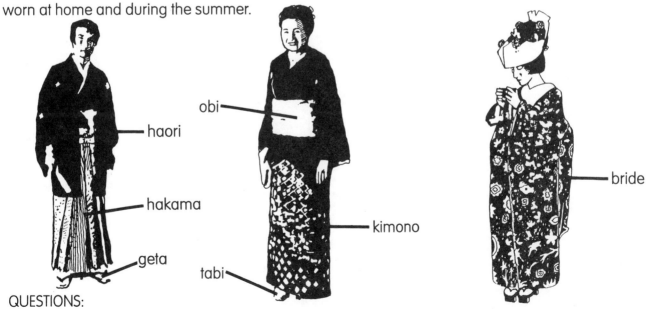

QUESTIONS:

1. For what reason do you think the Japanese continue to wear their traditional dress?

2. How has the clothing of our past changed? Why?

Copyright © 1992, Good Apple

51

Fashions–Then and Now

ACTIVITY:

You are going on a first-class five-day trip to Japan. Find out what the weather will be like. Keeping the weather in mind, plan everything you will need to bring and write them below. Go through catalogs, newspapers, and magazines. Cut out the items for your trip. Sketch the things you need but cannot find. Write down where you plan to go, what you plan to do, how you will dress for each activity and why. Plan to wear the traditional clothing at least once. Think about clothing, toiletries, accessories, cameras, undies, and such. Glue each day's items on construction paper. Decorate a suitcase cover and staple the six pages together. Now you are ready to go on an imaginary trip to Japan.

DAY 1   DAY 2

DAY 3

DAY 4   DAY 5

Copyright © 1992, Good Apple

GA1418

Seven Gods of Good Fortune

Many interesting customs and legends surround the Japanese New Year. The house is never swept on the first day of the new year because all of the good luck might be swept out.

A smile should be on every Japanese face because the expression a person displays on New Year's Day is the disposition he or she would like to have throughout the year.

The dream on the night of January 2nd is the first dream of the new year. A dream can tell what your fate will be. If you dream the same dream twice, it will tell you your future. The best and most desirable dream is the Takara-bune. It is about a treasure ship that the seven gods of wealth and happiness ride on. They each have their own unique treasures to give to you.

1. HOTEI (hoe-tie)—God of Happiness
2. JUROJIN (joo-row-gin)—God of Longevity
3. DAIKOKU (die-co-coo)—God of Wealth
4. BENZAITEN (ben-sigh-ten)—Goddess of Beauty
5. BISHAMOTEN (bee-sha-mon-ten)—Goddess of Dignity
6. EBISU (eh-bee-soo)—God of Abundance
7. FUKUROKUJU (foo-coo-row-coo-joo)—God of Wisdom

QUESTION:

What is your most memorable dream or nightmare? Can you give some reasons for dreaming that particular dream? Have you dreamed that same dream before?

ACTIVITY:

Using one or more of the seven gods, write a dream about them visiting you. Use numerous descriptive phrases. Design the magical ship they will be on board.

Copyright © 1992, Good Apple

GA1418

Seven Gods of Good Fortune

_____

_____

_____

_____

_____

_____

_____

_____

_____

_____

_____

_____

_____

_____

_____

_____

_____

Copyright © 1992, Good Apple

GA1418

Arts and Crafts of Japan

Japan has many art forms. Cloisonne´ is an art form where birds, people and flowers are painted on metal using copper and silver enamel and then baked at very high temperatures.

Dolls play an important part in the life of the Japanese. Warrior dolls are displayed during the colorful Boy's Day Festival (also known as Children's Day) on May 5th. Lovely Hina dolls are shown during Girl's Day on March 3rd. All of the dolls are handed down from generation to generation. They are never played with but are instead collected. The girls have tea parties on this special day.

Kokeshi are the traditional dolls made in the northeastern regions. They have a cylindrical body. Two or three colors (generally red, blue or yellow) are used to paint line or chrysanthemum designs on the body.

Lacquerware is a crafted article that has a shiny red or black lacquered finish. Numerous layers are brushed on and dried. Boxes and free-standing screens are the most common lacquerware items.

Watercolors are done on silk or Japanese paper. Scenes from nature are usually depicted.

Sumi-e painting is black ink and brush painting on a white background. It takes years to become a master at this.

The Ukiyo-e color print was perfected by Mononobu Hishikawa. The method was to carve a block of wood into a design. Paint was then applied over the block and paper was placed upon it to pick up the paint. Many colors were used on one wood-block print. Each color was washed off the wood, and a new color was applied and the process was repeated.

Origami is the art of paper folding. No scissors are used. Colorful squares of paper can be folded into birds, flowers, animals and other objects. This art is usually handed down from one generation to the next, just as dolls are.

Each family has its own mon (family crest design). It can be found on the front, back and sleeves of the men's formal kimono. The Japanese put this mon on furniture and accessories just like we put our initials on things. The mon custom has been around since the eighth century.

Some other art forms include ceramics, kite making, wood carving, paper cuts, embroideries, sculpturing and lantern making.

Copyright © 1992, Good Apple

Arts and Crafts of Japan

Mon Kiri
Paper Cutting

MATERIALS:

    Cut a 6" (15.24 cm) circle of white ditto paper.
    Cut a 6" (15.24 cm) square of black construction paper.
    Cut a 7" (17.78 cm) square of red construction paper.
    Cut an 8" (20.32 cm) square of black construction paper.
    glue
    scissors
    pencil

ACTIVITY:

1. Cut out the white circle.

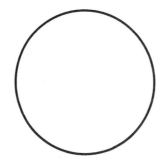

2. Fold in half.

3. Fold in thirds.

4. Fold in half again. Draw a design that will be easy to cut with the type of scissors available. NO LINES SHOULD TOUCH AND ALL DESIGNS MUST TOUCH THE OUTER EDGES.

5. Lightly shade in the areas to be cut out and cut.

6. Open the design and glue it on the 6" (15.24 cm) black paper. Glue this onto the 7" (17.78 cm) red paper. Lastly, glue that onto the 8" (20.42 cm) black paper. This makes a great Father's Day gift for Dad or Grandpa.

Copyright © 1992, Good Apple

GA1418

Tanabata Matsuri

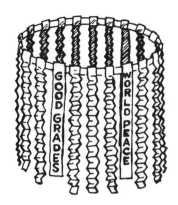

Tanabata Matusuri means "Star Festival." Sendai City has spectacular decorations for this festival. It is celebrated for three days (August 6-8). Bamboo poles fly overhead with brilliantly colored papers and plastic streamers of different designs and shapes. They hang from store fronts and are sometimes as long as two stories high.

The festival celebrates the story of two lovers in the night sky. The man is a shepherd, and the woman is a weaver (Vega and Altair). They lived across the Milky Way and were allowed to meet each other only once a year (on the eighth day of the eighth month).

QUESTION:

What astronomical event takes place around that time that may be the reason for this event? Research may be necessary.

MATERIALS:
> pastel construction paper cut in a circle (use a 33 rpm record)
> pastel crepe paper—$\frac{1}{2}$" (1.25 cm) wide and the length of the pack-
> > age of paper—one of five different colors for each student
> glue
> scissors
> four strips of construction paper 1" x 18" (2.54 x 45.72 cm)

ACTIVITY:
1. Trace around the record on the construction paper and cut.
2. Leave the crepe paper folded. Cut it in $\frac{1}{2}$" (1.25 cm) widths.
3. Open up crepe paper when cut. Fold in half and in half again. Cut so you have four strips of one color.
4. Squeeze and twist crepe paper strips with thumb and index finger from one end to the other.
5. Repeat for all five colors, four strips of each color.
6. Write wishes for peace or things you cannot buy, for their family, on the four construction paper strips. Be creative.
7. Students may use the five colors they have, or they may trade to create a new pattern of color. Glue them evenly around the circle of construction paper.
8. Hang them from the ceiling.

Copyright © 1992, Good Apple

GA1418

"Nip-Pon These"

In Japan there is a game called One Hundred Poems. It is a very old game taught to Japanese children so they can memorize important and famous poetry. One half of the poem is written on one card and the other half is written on a second card. The object of the game is to match the cards and collect the most pairs.

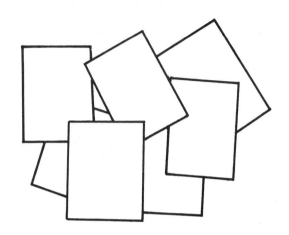

Students can make their own poetry cards in the same manner, or they can make up a twenty-question and twenty-answer card game using important or interesting facts about Japan. This is a good way to test knowledge of Japan.

MATERIALS:
    41–3" x 5" (7.62 x 12.7 cm) index cards
    pencil
    books and brochures on Japan
    encyclopedia to verify facts
    colored marker
    poetry books

ACTIVITY:
1. Each student makes up twenty well-written and challenging questions about Japan. They may be on any aspect of the Japanese culture. The answers must be correct and perhaps verified by two other students or the teacher.
2. Do not allow any questions that require a yes or no answer. No two questions should have the same answer.
3. Correctly print the questions on the question cards and the answers on the answer cards.
4. Write the game directions and object of the game on the single card that is left.
    a. All cards are placed facedown.
    b. Player selects two cards and puts them back, facedown, if the question and the answer do not match.
    c. If they do match, the player keeps the pair.
    d. Each player, in turn, does the same.
    e. Each player tries to get as many pairs as possible to win.
5. Decorate the tops of the cards in an identical design. Keep the designs simple.
6. Play the game with a friend.
7. These cards make a nice gift for a brother or sister.

Copyright © 1992. Good Apple

GA1418

Blockbuster Board Games

MATERIALS:

file folder	gameboard
game markers	die (dice)
index cards	library pocket for game cards
plastic bag for pieces	markers
construction paper	glue

ACTIVITY:

1. Form cooperative learning teams (2-3 students).
2. Brainstorm different aspects of Japan that you feel might work as a theme for a board game. Examples: food, clothing, government, holidays, etc.
3. Decide on a format for your game or base it loosely on one that is familiar.
4. As a group, write the basic rules for the game. Please include
   a. number of players
   b. object of the game
   c. who wins
   d. four to six simple sentences explaining the game
5. Decide the type of gameboard you would prefer or use the one with this lesson. Some other examples are

    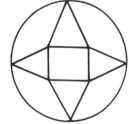 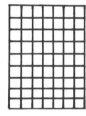

6. Assign jobs to team members.
7. Make the rough drafts and try the game out. Is it too complicated? Does it run smoothly and fairly? Does it make sense? Does it stick to the theme?
8. Make the final copies of all parts to the game (check your spelling, punctuation and capital letters).
9. Give the game a creative and extraordinary name.
10. Color everything.
11. Glue the gameboard on the right-hand side, inside the file folder. Laminate the folder, if you like, at this point.
12. Glue the library pocket on the inside, left (for game cards).
13. Glue a Ziploc bag on the inside (for game pieces and dice).
14. Play all the games at a Blockbuster Board Game Blastoff.

Copyright © 1992, Good Apple

GA1418

Blockbuster Board Games

START

END

Copyright © 1992, Good Apple

GA1418

Footloose and Fancy-Free Filmstrips

Japan has many tourist attractions and places to visit. Among these are castles, temples, famous cities, monuments, lakes, mountains, museums, cultural events, festivals, shrines, gardens, craft makers, shops, art galleries, parks and sporting events.

The best way to see Japan is to hop on board the "bullet trains" that are among the fastest and most extensive in the world. Wonderful meals are served on board, and you can taste food from several regions of Japan, all in one day.

As you studied about Japan hopefully you got a "feel" for the people, their customs, clothing, food, homes, holidays, festivals, language, religion, transportation, population, problems, technology, geography, cities, economy, plants and animals.

QUESTIONS:

1. Upon completion of this Japan study, name the five things that have impressed you the most about the country and give a reason for each impression.
2. What do you perceive as Japan's top three problems? What facts led you to these conclusions?

As a culminating activity, you will take an "arm chair" look around at the people, their lives and the country of Japan, all via filmstrips.

ACTIVITY:

From the topics listed above, select thirteen of your favorites. These will be used for your filmstrip frame pictures, which you will draw, and for the filmstrip dialogue, which you will write. Cut out the filmstrip form and glue it together. Next, write the title and put your name, as director, on the filmstrip. Draw one picture for each topic. Be thoughtful in your choices. Color the pictures and outline everything in fine-line black marker for greater clarity. Write one highly descriptive and entertaining sentence for each frame, including the introduction and ending. Talk about the most important facts only. Find some Japanese music. Play it in the background as you record the dialogue. Tap a glass gently with a knife to create a sound indicating it will be time to go on to the next frame. Make a filmstrip projector from a box. Store the filmstrip in a 35mm film can. Put a label on it.

Have a Footloose and Fancy-Free Filmstrip Festival.

Copyright © 1992, Good Apple

GA1418

Footloose and Fancy-Free Filmstrips

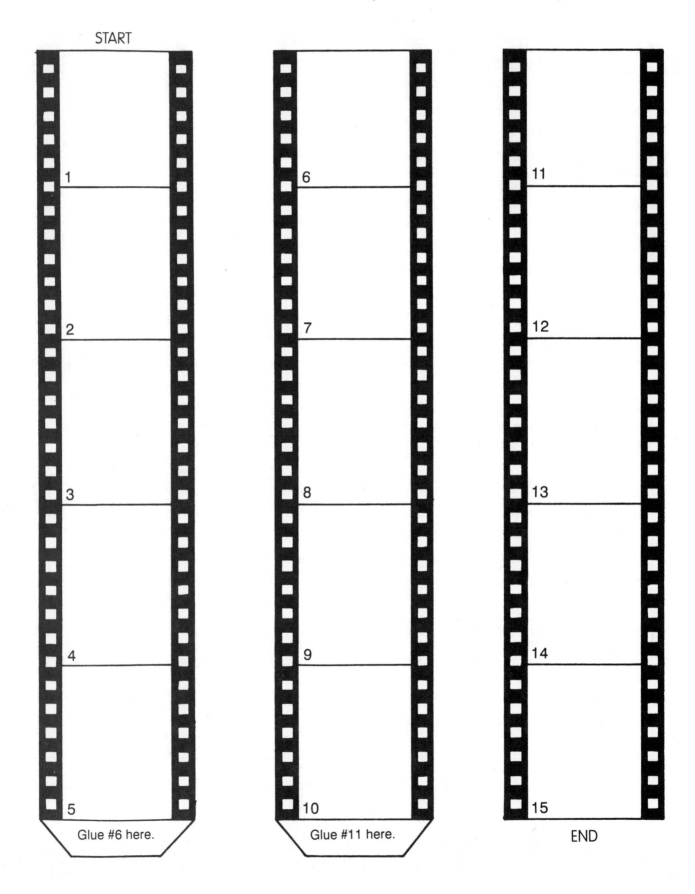

START

1

2

3

4

5

Glue #6 here.

6

7

8

9

10

Glue #11 here.

11

12

13

14

15

END

Copyright © 1992, Good Apple

GA1418